Receiving
POWER
from God

Andrew MURRAY

Whitaker House

Scripture quotations are taken from the *King James Version* (KJV) of the Bible.

RECEIVING POWER FROM GOD

(Previously titled *Living to Please God* and *Obtain the Power of God*)

ISBN: 0-88368-647-3
Printed in the United States of America
© 1984 by Whitaker House

Whitaker House
30 Hunt Valley Circle
New Kensington, PA 15068

2 3 4 5 6 7 8 9 10 11 12 / 09 08 07 06 05 04 03 02 01

CONTENTS

PREFACE

A number of years ago I was asked to write a series of articles encouraging Christians to live a life of earnest devotion to God. At that time I was deeply involved in a study of the epistle to the Ephesians. I thought I could connect the teaching of the epistle with my thoughts on spiritual living to give some help for the believer's quiet time with the Lord.

I am deeply conscious of my imperfections in expressing what I have seen of the treasures God has stored in this epistle for His Church. Nevertheless, I have compiled my thoughts in this book in the hope that God may use them to help some of His children realize the standard of the true Christian life. God is able and willing to make all the spiritual blessings and power that Paul's letter contains come true in our experience.

I send this book out with the prayer of Paul in his epistle, "That the God of our Lord Jesus Christ, the Father of glory, may give unto you the spirit of wisdom and revelation in the knowledge of him" (Ephesians 1:17). Unless that Spirit is sought, received, and yielded to, the truths of the epistle will remain a mystery. With the Spirit's teaching, we will "be filled with the knowledge of his will in all wisdom and spiritual understanding" (Colossians 1:9). We will discover that His power is actually able to do in us far above what we can ask or think.

Andrew Murray

Chapter 1

THE SPIRIT OF DEVOTION

"Pray to thy Father which is in secret; and thy Father. . .shall reward thee openly" (Matthew 6:6).

We use the word devotion in two ways—with regard to prayer in our private devotions and with regard to that spirit of devotion, or devotedness to God, which is to mark our daily life. If we meet our Father in the inner chamber, He will give us the open reward of grace to live our life to His glory and devote our whole being to His will. The *act of devotion* secures the power for that *spirit of devotion* which is to fill our daily life to His glory.

The classic passage on the law of devotion is Leviticus 27:28: "No devoted thing, that a man shall devote unto the Lord. . .shall be sold or redeemed: every devoted thing is most holy unto the Lord." Devotion is the wholehearted and irrevocable giving up to God of something which may never be taken back again. The person or thing becomes *most holy to the Lord*.

Aids to devotion may be given in more than one way. The simplest would be to suggest helpful ways to prepare us for worshipping God in truth. We could discuss some of the chief hindrances to effective prayer and Bible study or some of the reasons that these hindrances have such power over us. We may read a series of Scripture meditations to strengthen faith. The Word will become a joy to us and give us the humble trust that our devotions are pleasing to God.

Another way is more difficult, but it has some advantages. It does not deal directly with the act of devotion, but with that spirit which is to rule us all day and fill every action with true devotion to God. The goal is to encourage the personal involvement of the worshipper, stirring him to inquire as to what is the true meaning of a life wholly given up to God, His will, and His glory. He may think of his successes or failures in the past and their causes. He can then determine the measure of effort and self-denial necessary to succeed in the pursuit of true devotion.

Learning To Think

The goal of a good teacher is to stimulate the mind of the pupil to action. When a pupil is awakened to realize his powers and led to taste the joy of victory over apparently insurmountable difficulties, he has been given the key to discover truths for himself. No one can do us a greater favor than stimulating our desire to seek with our whole heart a spirit of life and devotion which is most pleasing to God.

Socrates has been called the greatest teacher (after Christ) the world has ever seen. He communicated no knowledge. He simply asked questions and helped his scholars to see their own ignorance and then to know their powers of thought and reason. Finally, he led them to understand that the real value of knowledge lay in its moral power, as the truth was received in the heart and life.

Today, men claim to have little time for personal meditation on divine truth. Perhaps we need a Socrates to awaken us by his questions to find out whether we really understand the words we use and honestly believe the truths we profess. The unbelieving Socrates could teach many Christians the meaning of true religion and help us in our devotion.

Our lives must be as holy as our prayers. Our prayers prove their reality by the fruit they bear in the holiness of our life. True devotion in prayer will assuredly be rewarded with the power to live a life of true devotion to Jesus and His service.

Let Jesus Christ Himself, our blessed Teacher, guide us to find out whether our devotion is what He desires from us—a full surrender to God and a full devotion to His glory every day.

Chapter 2

THE NEW TESTAMENT STANDARD

"Howbeit for this cause I obtained mercy, that in me first Jesus Christ might shew forth all long-suffering, for a pattern to them which should hereafter believe on him" (1 Timothy 1:16).

In any judgment we make, everything depends on our standard of measure. Many believers become content with the levels of ordinary Christianity. Although they may acknowledge that their own devotion is defective, there will be no deep conviction of sin or of the need and the possibility of any higher attainment.

But when we begin to see the standard of the New Testament and its universal obligation, we realize how far we have come short of it. We become convicted of the great sin of unbelief in the power of Jesus to keep us from sin and to enable us to walk pleasing to God. However impossible the standard is with men, it is not impossible with God because He works in us by the power of His Holy Spirit.

To discover the New Testament standard of devotion is not an easy matter. Our preconceived opinions blind us, and our environment exercises a powerfully deluding influence. Unless there is a sincere desire to know the whole will of God along with a prayerful dependence on the Holy Spirit's teaching, we may search in vain. But everyone who is truly willing to live entirely for God and desires in everything to please Him should be of good courage. God wants us to know His will and has promised by the Spirit to reveal it to us.

Paul—Our Example

Paul tells us that Christ made him a pattern for all believers, and he frequently admonishes the Churches to follow his example. In studying true New Testament devotion, Paul makes an excellent pattern. Why should we imitate Paul when God gave His Son as our perfect pattern? Many look upon Christ in His sinless perfection as utterly beyond what we can attain. Thus, His example loses much of its impact.

But Paul, the chief of sinners, is a man like us. Christ proved what He could do for a sinner in saving Paul and keeping him from sin. What Christ has done for Paul, He can and will do for us, too. If Christians made a careful study of the life of devotion Christ enabled Paul to live, we would be one step nearer to the absolute devotion to God set before us in Scripture. We would know the true devotion that is essential to a true Christian life.

Is there really a great difference between the standard of devotion in our churches and that of the New Testament? Our creeds honor God's Word, and we acknowledge Scripture as our only guide. A little reflection will suggest the answer. Not long after the first generations of Christians had passed away, terrible corruptions entered into the Church. In course of time, the Church sank into the darkness of the Middle Ages. With the Reformation and the preaching of the doctrine of justification by faith, there was a great revival of Christian truth. But it lacked the corresponding revival of Christian life and practice. While we bless God for the Reformation, we must remember that *it was not Pentecost.* The spirit and power of Pentecost was infinitely greater.

Church history tells us that it sometimes took half a century and more before some of the great doctrines of our faith were fully understood and formulated. It was not given to one generation to develop more than one truth at a time. All the strength of the Reformers was required to free the great doctrine of justification by faith from the errors under which it had been buried. The full exposition of the doctrine of sanctification, of the power and work of the Holy Spirit, of the calling of the Church to preach the gospel to the heathen—these truths were left to later ages.

Even now in studying the true standard of spiritual devotion to God, we must beware of looking to the Reformation or to later ages for our answer.

Our only safety is in careful study guided by the Holy Spirit and the teaching of Scripture. God gave Paul as an example and a pledge of what He could do for us. Therefore, we may be sure that his example of devotion, self-sacrifice, joy, and victory will help us find the path in which we can live pleasing to God.

Stepping Into Spiritual Life

Private devotions give us a clearer insight into what God is absolutely willing to do for us. A life prepared for us by God Himself is waiting to be revealed in us by the Holy Spirit. We must only be ready to know and confess how much is lacking in our spiritual life.

The Church today is characterized by the feeble workings of the Holy Spirit. The Bible promises us the mighty working of God's Spirit in the hearts of His children. Therefore, we should make a penitent confession of how little we have honored the Holy Spirit and lived up to what He is willing to work in us. Then our hearts will be drawn out to a new and stronger faith in the mighty workings of the Spirit which God has promised. Each day our devotions lead us out of the human standard we have been content with and into a life in the Spirit that God has provided and will certainly make real to us.

As we pursue our study, let us fix our attention on three simple questions:

1. Does Scripture really lay down a standard for

those who wholly yield themselves to the Spirit and trust God's almighty power to work in them?

2. Is it true that the Church as a whole does not live up to the standard that God has placed within our reach?

3. Are we ready to yield ourselves with our whole heart to accept what God has prepared?

Chapter 3

FINISHED AND UNFINISHED WORK

"Because ye are sons, God hath sent the Spirit of his Son into your hearts, crying, Abba, Father" (Galatians 4:6).

When God revealed His love for us in the gift of His Son, His great work was completed. When Christ was raised from the dead and seated on the throne of God, His work was also completed. The dispensation of the Spirit had begun.

The Spirit's job is to reveal all that the work of God and Christ had prepared. The work of the Holy Spirit has not yet been fully accomplished. For this reason, Christ sits upon the throne, waiting for all His enemies to be made His footstool. The work of the Father and the Son was finished when salvation was prepared for man's acceptance. The office of the Holy Spirit is to impart the grace which enables men to live out what the Father and the Son have provided.

In this dispensation, the Spirit's work and man's work are linked together. The Spirit does His work through man, and whatever is to be done in the Kingdom of God is done by man. The Holy Spirit can manifest Himself in no other way than in the spirit of man. In this dispensation we are to fulfill man's part in carrying out God's plan.

God's Glorious Plan

When Paul spoke of God in Christ reconciling the world to Himself, he immediately adds, "And hath committed unto us the word of reconciliation" (2 Corinthians 5:19). The responsibility of making the reconciliation known was entrusted to the Church. The power that reconciliation works in the world depends on the faithfulness or failure of God's people. These thoughts suggest the glory of the ministry of the Spirit, the terrible failure on the part of the Church, and the great need of restoration.

God's reason for sending the Spirit of Christ to take possession of the hearts of men was to restore their fellowship with Himself. All the work of God and Christ in redemption culminated in this one thing—the Holy Spirit was to communicate the salvation that had been provided and maintain unbroken fellowship in the heart of God's children. He was to be the Spirit of life, leading them in the path of holiness and perfect conformity to Jesus Christ. He was to be the Spirit of power, preparing them for service as Christ's witnesses to the ends of the earth. The Holy Spirit was to be the perfect bond of union between the Father in

16

heaven and the children on earth and between Christ and the perishing world.

In the power of the Spirit, every believer would be able to give his testimony of the love that had come to him. God's great purpose was that man should be saved by the witness of the men in whom He lived. The gift of the Spirit made this possible for everyone who yielded himself to God.

The Church has failed in its high calling. How few there have been who, with Paul, have proved that absolute dependence on the Spirit secures the continual presence and working of God in a Christian's life. Long prayers are offered for the power of the Holy Spirit, but few are ready to yield to His control. They do not know the secret of coming under His full power—the faith that dies to self and counts on God to do His perfect work. When the Church and the believer begin to understand this, there will be hope for the true revival of the Spirit in divine power.

Temples Of The Spirit

The Spirit has been poured out. He is yearning over us, and He is ready and able to take possession of His Church. Let us be ready to confess honestly the current state of the Church and the share we have in it. Let all who believe in the love and almighty power of God proclaim that God is longing to fill His redeemed people with the power of the Spirit. God will manifest Himself to all who are longing to be temples of the Holy

Spirit, filled with His power, and ready for the service of the living God.

What is the connection between the indwelling Spirit and the devotion of daily life? Our aim in our secret devotions must be to cast aside the ordinary standard of religion and make God's standard our unceasing desire. The Spirit has been given to us to reveal Christ and His life in us. No true progress can be made until we choose to live in unceasing dependence on the power of the Spirit in every area of our lives.

We must avoid the great hindrances along the way. We need to realize God's right to have absolute control of our lives. Our faith in His gracious and tender love will accomplish His work of power in our hearts. Ignorance of the power of the world as the great enemy of the blessed Spirit is dangerous. Unwillingness to take up the cross of Christ and follow Him can only be overcome by the Spirit. We must maintain that deep conviction of what a holy and almighty work it is for the Holy Spirit to take possession of our life and carry out His one desire—to make Christ live within us.

This great work is carried and accomplished in our daily devotions. With God's help, we will grow strong in faith, giving glory to God, trusting in Him to carry out His work in us. The goal of God in the gift of the Holy Spirit was to enable His people to become what they could never become in the Old Testament.

God does not expect us to strengthen and maintain our own spiritual life. That is the work of His Holy Spirit. Only the soul who lives in entire surrender to and dependence on the blessed Spirit can effectually carry on God's mighty work and accomplish all His blessed purposes.

Chapter 4

EXPERIENCING LIFE IN HIM

"Blessed be the God and Father of our Lord Jesus Christ, who hath blessed us with all spiritual blessings in all heavenly places in Christ" (Ephesians 1:3).

A study of the letter to the Ephesians will help us discover the New Testament standard of devotion. The opening words of the epistle not only give us a blessed summary of the truth of the gospel, but they reveal, out of the depths of Paul's experience, what the true Christian life is.

First let us consider the grace of our Lord Jesus Christ. The God and Father of our Lord Jesus Christ has blessed us with all spiritual blessings *in Him*. The expression *in Him* is the keynote of the epistle, occurring more than twenty times.

The words of our text are the beginning of a sentence which continues through verse 14. We find we are chosen in Him, foreordained through Him, accepted in Him, and redeemed in Him. The purpose of God is in Him, and all things are summed up and "made into an heritage in Him." In Him we believed, and in Him we were sealed with the Holy Spirit. All our blessings are treasured up in Christ, and we are in Him, too. As truly as the blessings are in Christ, so truly is our life in Him—the two are inseparably intertwined. Abiding in Christ means abiding in the heavenly places and in all the spiritual blessings God has given us in Him.

Faith in Christ is meant to be nothing less than unceasing dependence upon Him and fellowship with Him. From Him we receive every grace the soul can possibly need. Your soul may be kept in blessed fellowship with Jesus as constantly as you live and breathe. This is what Scripture means by the words, "Christ, who is our life" (Colossians 3:4), "Christ liveth in me" (Galatians 2:20), "To me to live is Christ" (Philippians 1:21). What riches of grace these are!

God's Gift Of Love

Christ was the Father's gift to us, and all blessings are given by Him. God's purpose was to bring us back to Himself as our Creator. Our happiness can be found in His fellowship and glory alone. God satisfied the love of His own heart by bringing us into complete union with Christ, so that in Him we can be as near to God as Christ is. Oh, the mystery of the love of God!

Our text says, "God has blessed us with all spiritual blessings." More than one believer has found in these words the key that unlocks the treasury of blessing. As the light of the Spirit shines on these words, they come alive with new meaning. In Christ, God *has* blessed me with all spiritual blessings. Faith and wholehearted surrender are free to claim them in Him, and the heart finds itself in the very center of blessing.

The revelation of the blessings and the faith that claims them lead to the adoring benediction—"Blessed be the God and Father of our Lord Jesus Christ!" It is the fountain from which the stream of blessings flows through the epistle. In our life, too, may it be an unceasing song of praise, "I will bless the Lord at all times: his praise shall continually be in my mouth" (Psalm 34:1).

Spiritual blessings are simply the blessings of the Holy Spirit. He has the divine office of imparting to us all the fullness of blessing and blessedness in the divine life. He reveals them to us. He enables us to see, delight in, and accept them. He communicates them to our heart, and we become spiritual men, clothed with the power of the Spirit.

Where the heart is fully yielded to Him, the Spirit does more than influence our thoughts and actions. He dwells within us in divine reality and power, making our heart the temple of Christ. He imparts every grace and virtue that is in Christ to us. The seed sown in the earth needs the warmth of the sun and the rain from heaven to make it grow. Even so, as we believe that the seeds of grace and virtue are within us, we look up to Christ in whom our life is. In the sunshine of His love, the spiritual blessings grow into our very being.

In the epistle, the Holy Spirit is mentioned twelve times in different aspects of the work He does in the believer. As we study these, we will find a wonderful revelation of what God meant the life of His children to be. If we desire to discover the New Testament standard of true spirituality and devotion in our life, we must have the courage to set aside every human standard and make God's purpose our only aim.

Begin With Praise

Let us begin by reading the benediction of the letter to the Ephesians. It reveals the true life of spiritual blessing, and we can try and make it our own. Let us, in quiet meditation, wait on the Holy Spirit to work faith in our innermost consciousness. As one whom the Father has blessed in Christ with every spiritual blessing, humbly take your place before Him and say, "Blessed be God! Blessed be God!"

People may complain about the lack of spiritual life and pray for its deepening. Yet much ignorance remains concerning what is really needed to bring a Christian into a strong and joyous life in Christ Jesus. Let us learn the lesson from our text that nothing less than the adoring worship of the blessed Trinity can meet our need. Our expecta-

23

tion is to rest upon God, who has blessed us in Christ Jesus. God and His blessings are found in Christ if we continue in close and unceasing fellowship with Him.

Through the Spirit, the presence of the Father and the Son in divine power can be known. The Holy Spirit has been given to make Christ real to us and to make every spiritual blessing ours. A life entirely given up to the Holy Spirit and a heart full of faith and confidence that God will do His wondrous work within us will see miracles. A body yielded to God as a holy, living sacrifice on the altar for His service will surely be accepted. God will teach us to sing the song of praise, "Blessed be the God and the Father of our Lord Jesus Christ, who has blessed us with all spiritual blessings in the heavenly places in Christ" (Ephesians 1:3).

Chapter 5

THE SEAL OF THE SPIRIT

"In whom also after that ye believed, ye were sealed with that holy Spirit of promise" (Ephesians 1:13).

The wonderful sentence that began in verse 3 listing the spiritual blessings we have in Christ closes with the blessed *sealing of the Holy Spirit.* When a king appoints an ambassador, his commission is sealed with the king's seal. The Holy Spirit Himself, by His life in us, is the seal of our sonship. His work is to reveal and glorify Christ in us, the image of the Father. By fixing our heart and our faith on Him, He transforms us into His likeness.

What a wonderful thought! The Spirit of the Father and the Son, the bond of union between them, comes to us as the bond of our union with them. He gives us the witness of the divine life within us and enables us to experience that life here on earth. In the Christian life, everything depends on knowing the Holy Spirit and His blessed work.

Lord Of All

First of all, we need to know that He comes to take the mastery of our whole being—spirit, soul, and body. Through it all, He reveals the life and the power of God as it works in our renewed nature. Christ could not be glorified and receive the Spirit from the Father for us until He died upon the cross and parted with the sin and weakness of our nature. Likewise, the coming of the Holy Spirit into our hearts in power implies that we must yield ourselves to the fellowship of the cross and consent to die to self and sin. Thus, through the Spirit, the new and heavenly life may take complete possession of us.

This entire mastery demands complete surrender and obedience on our part. Peter speaks of the "Holy Ghost, whom God hath given to them that obey him" (Acts 5:32). Christ humbled Himself to the perfect obedience of the cross that He might receive the Spirit from the Father for us. In the same way, our full experience of the Spirit's power rests entirely on our readiness to deny self and yield ourselves to His teaching and leading.

The reason that believers are feeble and ignorant of the blessings of the Spirit is that they never made a decision to yield themselves to the control of the Spirit at every moment. Pray that God's children might accept God's terms—complete mastery of the Spirit and the unhesitating surrender of the whole being to His control.

We especially need to understand that the degree in which the working of the Spirit is experienced may vary greatly. A believer may rejoice in one of the gifts of the Spirit, such as peace or boldness, and still be extremely deficient in other areas. Our attitude toward the Spirit must be that of perfect teachableness, waiting to be led by Him into the will of God. We must realize how much there still is within the heart that needs to be renewed and sanctified if He is to have the place and honor that belong to Him.

The Spirit's Transforming Power

Two great enemies obtained dominion over man when Adam sinned—the world and self. Of the world Christ says, "The Spirit of truth; whom the world cannot receive, because it seeth him not, neither knoweth him" (John 14:17). Worldliness is the great hindrance that keeps believers from living a spiritual life. Of self Christ said, "Let him deny himself" (Mark 8:34). Self, in all its forms—self-will, self-pleasing, self-confidence—renders life in the power of the Spirit impossible.

Nothing can deliver us from these two great enemies except the cross of Christ. Paul boasts in the cross by which he has been crucified to the world. He tells us, "They that are Christ's have crucified the flesh" (Galatians 5:24). To live the spiritual life, we must completely give up the old life to

27

make room for the blessed Spirit. He will then be free to renew and transform our whole being into the will of God.

Without the Spirit, we can do nothing acceptable to God. "No man can say that Jesus is Lord, but by the Holy Ghost" (1 Corinthians 12:3). No man can truly say, "Abba, Father" except by the Spirit of God's Son sent into our hearts. In our fellowship with God and with men, in our religious worship and our daily vocations, in the highest pursuit that life can offer and in the daily care of our bodies—everything must bear the seal of the Holy Spirit.

Of the Son we read, "Him hath God the Father sealed" (John 6:27). We are sealed *in Christ*. When the Spirit descended upon Jesus at His baptism, He was led by the Spirit to the wilderness and led through His whole life to the cross. "Through the eternal Spirit offered himself without spot to God" (Hebrews 9:14). We, too, are to live daily as those who are sealed by the Spirit.

The words, "Him hath God the Father sealed," are true of every believer. The Son and every son have been sealed by the Father. The New Testament standard of the Christian life and its devotion is that everything we do bears the stamp of the Holy Spirit.

The Holy Spirit cannot inspire our devotion, unless He inspires our daily life. The Spirit of Christ must rule the whole man if He is to perform His blessed work in us. The indwelling of the Holy

Spirit means that nothing is to be thought of, trusted, or sought after except continual dependence on His blessed work.

The way we live our daily life will be the test of the sincerity of our heart's devotion. As we mature spiritually, our confidence in God who works in us through His blessed Spirit will grow. Every thought of faith in the power of the Spirit must find its expression in prayer to God. He will surely give us His Spirit when we ask Him to work in us what we need.

A seal attached to a document gives validity to every word it contains. Even so, the Holy Spirit of promise who sealed us also ratifies every promise that is in Christ. This is one of the great differences between the Bible and the human standard of the Christian life. In the Bible, the seal of the Spirit is accepted in His control of every movement and every moment of our life. By human standards, we are content with sadly partial surrender to His guidance.

Chapter 6

THE SPIRIT OF WISDOM

"Making mention of you in my prayers; That. . .the Father of glory, may give unto you the spirit of wisdom and revelation in the knowledge of him: The eyes of your understanding being enlightened; that ye may know" (Ephesians 1:16-18).

Immediately after Paul mentioned the Holy Spirit as God's seal on believers, he spoke of his unceasing prayer that God would give them the spirit of wisdom. It is not enough that the believer has the Holy Spirit. The Spirit can only do His work in answer to prayer.

Paul prayed unceasingly and teaches us to pray unceasingly, too, for the wisdom of the Spirit to enlighten the eyes of our heart. Just as a child needs education, the believer who has the Spirit within him needs divine illumination daily to know God and the spiritual life He bestows. Without spiritual wisdom and understanding, we can never comprehend it.

Knowing Hope, Riches, And Power

Paul lists three things that we need to know: 1. "The hope of his calling"—the holy calling in which we are to walk. 2. "The riches of the glory of his inheritance in the saints"—the unsearchable riches of the heavenly treasure which God has in His saints. 3. The power by which we can fulfill our calling and possess our heritage—"the exceeding greatness of his power to us-ward who believe." (See Ephesians 1:18-19.)

This passage teaches many valuable lessons for those who are in the ministry. It points to the three great spiritual blessings that include all a Christian needs to know of what God has prepared for him. They remind us that to preach these truths to believers is not sufficient because human wisdom cannot grasp them.

If the knowledge is to come alive and be effective, it needs a special illumination of the Holy Spirit. Only the spiritual man can discover spiritual things. God Himself, the Father of glory, will give the Spirit of wisdom in answer to definite and persevering prayer. Such teaching and praying will lead believers to the full life which the letter to the Ephesians sets before them.

The life of the Christian is truly the life of God in the soul. Nothing that we do can maintain that life or renew it. The great need of the believer is to wait upon God for the Holy Spirit to show "the exceeding greatness of his power to us-ward who believe." No human mind can grasp it. The Holy Spirit living in the heart reveals it and teaches us to believe this truth. As Christians we are to depend on God every day to work in us according to the greatness of His strength in us who believe. When we accept the Holy Spirit's teaching in answer to prayer, He will keep us conscious of this mighty power working in us.

Obtaining The Power

The Holy Spirit shows us the work and nature of the mighty power dwelling within us. It is the power of God, "according to the working of his mighty power, Which he wrought in Christ, when he raised him from the dead, and set him at his own right hand" (Ephesians 1:19-20). This power works in us who believe and raises us from the power of death to a life in the glory of heaven. By the greatness of this power, our daily life may be lived in fellowship with the Son of God.

God raised Christ from the dead because His death on the cross exhibited deep humility and perfect obedience. Because Jesus yielded Himself unreservedly to the power of God, He was raised from the dead and given glory. When we give ourselves over to die with Christ to sin and the world in humility and obedience, God will make us partakers of the resurrection power and of the Spirit of glory.

The life of the believer as an exhibition of the greatness of God's power is a theme that runs through all the writings of Paul. In his prayer for the Colossians, he asks that they may "walk worthy of the Lord unto all pleasing, being fruitful in every good work, and increasing in the knowledge of God; Strengthened with all might according to his glorious power, unto all patience and long-suffering with joyfulness" (Colossians 1:10-11).

As one thinks of the life of devotion which Paul describes—always worthy of God and pleasing to Him—one feels that the standard is impossible. But then the thought comes in, "Strengthened with all might according to his glorious power," and we say, "No, if this is true, if God works this, the life is possible."

These same thoughts occur in Ephesians 3:20-21, "Now unto him that is able to do exceeding abundantly above all that we ask or think, according to the power that worketh in us, Unto him be glory." These words lift our heart to believe and expect something far beyond what we ask or think. The life we are to live is to be a supernatural one—the resurrection life. We experience the heavenly life of Christ in glory maintained in us by the same working of the strength of His might which raised Christ from the cross to the throne.

The same almighty power which raised Christ from the dead as the conqueror of sin and death is the power that works in our hearts to give us victory over every sin. To believe this with our whole heart will immediately bring a sense of our own weakness, but we will also know with divine certainty that God will fulfill His purpose in us.

Reigning In Him

If the believer trusts the greatness of God's power and yields himself in entire subjection to let that power rule in his heart; if he will be content to trust the strength that is made perfect in weakness and count all things loss for the sake of this blessed prize; then God's Word is pledged that the power that raised Christ will work in him day by day until he knows what it means to live and reign with Christ in glory.

We are trying to grasp the New Testament standard of a life of true devotion and whether the accepted standard of our modern Christianity is in harmony with it. Try to realize the full meaning of Paul's prayer. Think of his private pleading for the Ephesians. Think of the standard of his own life as he speaks of God working in him. Think of what he wished his readers to take as their aim and expectation. Paul's heart was set upon two goals for every believer—to live every day under the teaching of the Holy Spirit and under the mighty power of God working in him.

Has your secret devotion, your confident faith, and your hope in daily life accepted and rejoiced in the life that is held out to you? Are you daily living out the greatness of God's power working in you as you yield yourself to the Holy Spirit and keep depending on His power?

May God help us to return again to this passage until it becomes to us the light of God shining in our heart and the power of God working in our life!

Chapter 7

DRAWING NEAR TO GOD

"Through him we both have access by one Spirit unto the Father" (Ephesians 2:18).

Christ and the Holy Spirit are united in a great work to make the permanent and unceasing presence of God become a blessed reality. Our text not only speaks of a *right* of access, but of its actual experience and enjoyment as provided for us through Christ and His Spirit.

Think of what Scripture teaches us. In the tabernacle, God dwelt in the Holy of Holies, separated by a thick veil from the priests who came daily to serve. Even the High Priest could enter that holy place only once every year. Access through the veil was forbidden on pain of death.

When Christ died, this veil was torn in two. Christ Jesus not only entered into God's presence with His blood, but He opened a new and living way through the torn veil of His flesh for us to enter, too. When Jesus entered heaven, the way was opened for every believer to enter into God's holy presence and dwell there every day. Jesus sent us the Holy Spirit to bring us into that holy presence and enable us to live there. The unbroken enjoyment of God's presence is available to every believer who is willing to forsake all to possess it.

Unified By The Son And Spirit

"Through the Son" means more than our Advocate who secures our acquittal and acceptance. Our High Priest lives and acts in the power of an endless, incorruptible life. He works in us through the power of His resurrection life and His entrance into glory. To have access to God through Christ means that we have been made alive with Christ and made to sit with Him in the heavenly places. (See Ephesians 2:5-6.) We live in Him, and we are one with Him. He keeps us in fellowship with God. The access through Christ brings us as near to God as Christ is, in intimate and divine fellowship.

The Spirit has been given to us that we may have the power to cry out to the Father, even as Christ did. The Spirit dwells in us to reveal Christ. Without Him, no man can say that Jesus is Lord. The Spirit takes possession of our whole life and being. When He is yielded to and trusted, He maintains our fellowship with the Father through the Son.

The New Testament standard of Christian living consists of access to God's holy presence and love through the living union with Christ in the power of the Holy Spirit. The one thing needed to make it ours is the practice of the presence of God. When we give up our own life, Christ's life may be carried out in us. Access through Christ in the Spirit will restore to us what Adam lost by sin.

A walk in the light of God can be as clear and natural as the enjoyment of feeling the warmth of the sun on our bodies. No thinking, feeling, or working can enable us to dispense with the daily privilege of access into the Holiest of all and of dwelling there.

Making An Impact On Your World

Most of us have heard the expression, "Take time to be holy." A missionary in China for more than twenty years often said to young missionaries, "Preach the gospel, and take time to be as holy as the preparation. The missionary must above everything else be a holy man. Unbelievers expect it of him. He must be more than a good person, and more than someone who takes time to master the language and the literature of the people. He must be holy.

"This is what we need if this world is to be moved by us. The throne of grace must be our refuge with the shadow of the Almighty as our dwelling place every hour. We must take time to be filled with His power. We must take time to be holy."

The person who takes time to fellowship with

God will become holy, too. The inner chamber is the school of true devotion.

Take time to be alone with the holy God. Take time with the Father, of whom it is said, "The very God of peace sanctify you wholly. . . .Faithful is he that calleth you, who also will do it" (1 Thessalonians 5:23-24).

Take time with Christ, the holy One of God, who said, "For their sakes I sanctify myself, that they also might be sanctified through the truth" (John 17:19).

Take time with the Holy Spirit who makes you His holy temple. Give time to this holy fellowship, and God Himself will sanctify you entirely. Live in unbroken fellowship because through Christ we have our access in one Spirit to the Father.

Chapter 8

SPIRITUAL BUILDING BLOCKS

"Jesus Christ himself being the chief corner stone; In whom all the building fitly framed together groweth unto an holy temple in the Lord: In whom ye also are builded together for an habitation of God through the Spirit" (Ephesians 2:20-22).

The blessed Trinity is mentioned here again—the Father for whom the habitation is built; Jesus Christ, the chief cornerstone; and the Spirit, the builder through whom all the living stones are united with each other in perfect fellowship with God.

The main point of our text is *fellowship*—the fellowship of the Spirit. That fellowship is spoken of first as the *fellowship of believers* who are built up into one holy temple. Paul spoke of the Gentiles as strangers from the covenant of the promise who are now accepted by the blood of Christ. The enmity between Jews and Gentiles was nailed to the cross that we *both* might have access in one Spirit to the Father.

In verse 19 he says, "Ye are no more strangers and foreigners, but fellowcitizens with the saints, and of the household of God." Jew and Gentile have access by one Spirit to the Father, and by the same Spirit, they are built up into one temple.

The cross has ended all separation among Jews and Gentiles, Greek and barbarian, the wise and the foolish—all are one in Christ Jesus. National and social distinctions cannot stand against the unity of the Spirit. The cement which holds the living stones together, the bond which makes all members of one household and one body is the Spirit and the life and the love of God Himself.

Our Bond Of Love

Our *fellowship with Christ,* the Cornerstone, is also the work of the Holy Spirit. In Him, the believer on earth and the Father in heaven find their bond of union. Men think of pardon, peace, obedience, and holiness as an end in themselves. But they are only means to the great end of bringing God and man into perfect union. We prize the atonement through the blood of Christ while we forget there is something higher—the presence and fellowship of God Himself.

God dwelt in the sanctuary in the midst of His people so that He could be their God. They enjoyed His guidance, His blessing, His mighty deliverance in their time of need, and His abiding presence. Fellowship with the Father and the Son, that intimate, holy, and unceasing communion, is the reason for man's creation. That fellowship has been restored to us in Christ Jesus.

As believers realize their dependence on Christ and their inseparable union with Him, they will trust the Spirit to maintain within them the faith of His presence. Then they will know that the presence and the power of God is the highest of all the blessings in Christ Jesus. Through the Spirit alone we can have access in Christ to the Father. He reveals Christ to us and the reality of our union with Him. We can experience the nearness to God He gives.

He not only builds the temple, but He reveals the indwelling God. He makes each heart a temple and reveals God's willingness to be and to do in our heart what He is and does in heaven above. It seems impossible to many Christians that the presence of God can be with them and keep them. But it is indeed possible if we know and believe in the Holy Spirit as the power of God that works in us.

Loving The Brethren

The fellowship with God, with Christ, and with other believers constitutes the blessedness of being built as a habitation of God in the Spirit. The cross of Christ destroyed all selfishness. The love that seeks no life but giving itself for others has been made available to us.

Close fellowship with each other is as sacred

and vital as our fellowship with God. Our spiritual life depends on it, and the only way of showing men our love for God and the reality of God's love for us is through our love for one another. Our Lord Jesus prayed, "That they all may be one. . . .that the world may know that thou. . .hast loved them, as thou hast loved me" (John 17:21,23). Jesus taught us that a divided church is powerless before the enemy. Only love for the brethren like God's and Christ's will give us the victory. The world will be compelled to acknowledge that Christ's love is present and working in us.

When the New Testament standard of spiritual life is lifted up and our love of the brethren proves the reality of our love for God, our life will conform to the image of Jesus. Our prayers will be delivered from the selfishness that often hinders them. Our hearts will feel a new confidence that God will hear our prayers for the growth of a holy temple in the Lord. God's presence with us and our devotion to Him can be the mark of our daily life.

Chapter 9

PROCLAIMING THE WAY OF LIFE

"The mystery of Christ. . .as it is now revealed unto his holy apostles and prophets by the Spirit; That the Gentiles should be fellowheirs, and of the same body, and partakers of his promise in Christ" (Ephesians 3:4-6).

The more one studies Paul's letter to the Ephesians, the deeper the impression becomes that the true standard of New Testament faith is faintly realized in the Church today. The tone of the letter is intensely supernatural. Only a life identified with the life of Christ and under the guidance of the Holy Spirit can grasp its full meaning.

In the first chapter, Paul set before us the *source* of the divine life. His unceasing prayer was that supernatural life would be revealed by the Holy Spirit in the heart of believers. In chapter two, we had the *communication* of that life. God made us alive in Christ, and we are His workmanship, created in Christ Jesus for good works.

Now, we are taught that the *proclamation* of

that divine life is also the work of God and His Spirit. As definitely as the origin and communication of His life is supernatural, so the provision for its being made known in the world is entirely supernatural, too. God's grace is set before us in a new light.

In chapter one we had "his grace wherein he hath made us accepted in the beloved. . .the forgiveness of sins, according to the riches of his grace" (Ephesians 1:6-7). In chapter two we had "the exceeding riches of his grace" (Ephesians 2:7). Now in chapter 3 we have "the dispensation of the grace of God which is given. . . .unto his holy apostles and prophets by the Spirit" (Ephesians 3:2,5). Paul was made a minister of this grace, "according to the gift of the grace of God by the effectual working of his power" (Ephesians 3:7).

In the ministry of the gospel, the riches of God's grace are greatly magnified. Paul speaks of the mystery of Christ and says it has now been revealed by the Holy Spirit. The Gentiles are fellow-heirs and fellow-partakers in Christ Jesus. Through the Spirit, the revelation of what had been hidden in God through the ages was revealed.

Led By The Spirit

Throughout the book of Acts, we read of the Spirit guiding the steps of Philip, Peter, Barnabas, and Paul. They spoke under the power and anoint-

45

ing of the Spirit, and many received the word with joy. The Holy Spirit was entrusted with the whole work of revealing and carrying out through the ages to come the riches of the glory of this mystery among the Gentiles—"Christ in you, the hope of glory" (Colossians 1:27).

All mission work has been placed under the direction of the Holy Spirit. In every area of that work, His guidance is to be sought and can be counted on. Missions are indeed the work of the Holy Spirit.

Why is so little use made of the language of Scripture in our evangelism today? The Holy Spirit will reveal the great mystery of God in the heart, awaken its affections and its purpose, and empower it with all that is needed to carry out God's blessed will. It is not enough that the Spirit reveals this hidden mystery of God to preachers so that through them the Church may become acquainted with His plans. Each believer needs to receive the teaching of the Spirit personally if the blessed secret is to master him.

Answering Our Call

We consider it a great step forward when a congregation yields itself to the call to take part in the great work of evangelizing the world. Yet this may come about from nothing more than a sense of duty and readiness to take part in all the activities of the Church. Believers must realize that missions are the chief aim of the Church, the one object for which every congregation and every believer exists. In preaching and in writing, in prayer and in Christian fellowship, all work within the Church should train her for her great calling— work on the mission field to win the unbelievers for Christ.

Dependence on the Holy Spirit is the first and essential element of success. By the Spirit, the Church will be able to carry out its Lord's commands. When the Holy Spirit takes the place that was given to Him in the early Church, we may expect His power to be manifested as it was in those days.

"Ye shall receive power, after that the Holy Ghost is come upon you: and ye shall be witnesses unto me. . .unto the uttermost part of the earth" (Acts 1:8). These were the last words of our Lord on the earth. The fullness of the Spirit will only be given in connection with the extension of the Kingdom. The power for carrying the gospel to those near or far depends on the measure of the Spirit's presence. Every prayer for the power of the Spirit to be revealed should have as its aim the power to testify for Jesus. As the number of believers increases who pray for the Spirit, the Church will become strong for preaching the gospel to every creature.

The School Of Prayer

A close connection exists between these thoughts and our life of secret devotion. Paul spoke to believers of the conflict he had in unceasing prayer for the churches who were struggling among the world of unbelievers. He asked them to strive with him in prayer for his work of preaching to the Gentiles. Prayer was not to be only for the supply of the needs of the spiritual life, but a training school for the exercise of the highest power available to us in God's service.

Prayer brings us into conflict with the powers of darkness and into fellowship with the cross. It stirs our strength to take hold of God and prevail with Him for His blessing on men around us. Prayer causes believers to realize, amid their deep sense of unworthiness and helplessness, "I have power with God. He will listen to me. He will cause our mission work to triumph through the power of the cross on the battlefield in the world."

Let us test the effectiveness of our prayers by the influence they exercise on the fulfillment of the mystery of Christ in the world. Work can be done in the prayer closet that will count for eternity. There, the power can be received that will make itself felt wherever God sends us to establish His Kingdom on earth. Let us not be afraid to say what Paul said of himself, "Unto me, who am less than the least of all saints, is this grace given, that I should preach among the Gentiles the unsearchable riches of Christ" (Ephesians 3:8).

We may count on God to lead us into the riches of the glory of this mystery among the Gentiles. Our prayer will be for the power of the Holy Spirit to permeate all that is being done for mission work in the Church and throughout the world.

Chapter 10

OPENING THE DOOR TO POWER

"I bow my knees unto the Father. . .that he would grant you, according to the riches of his glory, to be strengthened with might by his Spirit in the inner man; That Christ may dwell in your hearts by faith" (Ephesians 3:14, 16-17).

We see in this wonderful prayer the harmonious work of the blessed Trinity. The Father grants the Spirit of power. The Spirit reveals Christ in the heart. Through Christ and the Spirit, we are filled with all the fullness of God! As God dwells in heaven as the Three in One, even so He lives in our hearts.

At the close of chapter one of Ephesians, we prayed for the Spirit of wisdom that we might know God in the greatness of His power to us who believe. Here we have the prayer for the Spirit of power to strengthen us with His might. The greatness of God's power is to be a permanent experience in our inner life. Let us bow with deep reverence as we gaze upon this mystery of love.

Notice first the expression, "That he would grant you, according to the riches of his glory." Paul wants us to take time and think of God's glory and inconceivable riches. Then, in faith, we can expect that God will do nothing less to us than according to the riches of that glory. Our inner man can experience the glory of God shining in our heart and manifesting His power in what He does within us. Our faith cannot expect the fulfillment of the prayer until it enters into and claims that God will work in us according to the riches of His glory. Let us take time and see that nothing less than this is the measure of our faith.

"That he would grant you. . .to be strengthened with might by his Spirit in the inner man." The Spirit is indeed the mighty power of God. As the Spirit of wisdom, He reveals the greatness of God's power in us who believe—the power that lifted Christ from the cross to the throne. He teaches us to believe in the greatness of God's power in us. As the Spirit of power, He works in us, strengthening us in the inner man.

In His Word, God continually calls on His servants to be strong and courageous. God chooses the weak things of this world, but He wants them to be strong in faith and strong in the power of His might. With strength of will, they can be ready to do all God says; and with strength of character, they will be bold for any sacrifice. In a healthy body, strength is not something separated from the whole, but it fills the entire being and permeates

51

every fiber. Likewise, to be strengthened with might by the Spirit in the inner man simply means that our whole being is under the sway of His mighty power.

Abiding In Christ

The object of this strengthening with might is that *Christ dwell in the heart by faith.* The divine power enables and emboldens our faith to claim this precious privilege. The Spirit reveals Christ dwelling within us and gives the consciousness of His unceasing and omnipotent presence.

Just as God maintains the life of the body by supporting the heart in its action, the Holy Spirit, by His almighty power, strengthens our inner man daily to enable us to live the true spiritual life. Christ's dwelling in the heart is meant to be our portion. In speaking of his conversion, Paul says, "It pleased God. . .to reveal his Son in me, that I might preach him among the heathen" (Galatians 1:15-16). When he preached the unsearchable riches of Christ, he preached Him as dwelling in the heart. He would have none of his readers to be without it. He continually pleaded with God to strengthen them with might in their inner life, so that nothing might keep them from this wonderful blessing.

It seems as if the Church has lost the understanding of the reality of Christ's indwelling. Yet Paul's teaching is in harmony with that of our blessed Lord. When Jesus spoke of the gift of the

Holy Spirit, He said, "At that day ye shall know that I am in my Father, and ye in me, and I in you" (John 14:20). He goes on to add, "If a man love me, he will keep my word and my Father will love him, and we will come unto him and make our abode with him" (John 14:23).

Our Lord speaks here of something far beyond the initial grace of pardon and regeneration. He speaks of what would be given to those who love Him and keep His commandments—of a special gift of the Holy Spirit dwelling and working in them. The blessing offered to us completes the spiritual life with the highest exhibition of what the mighty power of God can work in us.

Christ wants to dwell in the heart. Let us begin with urgent prayer for ourselves and for God's children around us. God will work according to the riches of His glory to lift us out of our feebleness and bring us into a new life that will be lived to His praise and glory.

When Jesus Christ is within us, we are *rooted and grounded in love.* We can begin to comprehend the reality and the joy of the love of Christ that passes knowledge. This leads to being filled with the fullness of God. The Spirit of power fills the inner man, the presence of Christ fills the heart, and the fullness of God fills all.

No wonder Paul says, "Now unto him that is able to do exceeding abundantly above all that we ask or think, according to the power that worketh in us, unto him be glory" (Ephesians 3:20-21).

Faith in the promise of what the Father of glory will do, according to the riches of His glory, will teach us to worship saying, "Glory! Glory to Him forever and ever."

Assured Of God's Mighty Power

This doxology gives a revelation of what lies at the root of Paul's standard of prayer and expectation. He was confident that his prayer that believers be strengthened with might in the inner man, according to the riches of God's glory, would be granted. Many say this was meant to be an ideal to stir our desires, but that its actual fulfillment in life in this world is beyond our reach. This thought cuts away the root of the faith in the supernatural power of God in our lives. Since it is absolutely secured in the promise, it is therefore possible in experience.

Paul dares any reader to say that what he asks for out of the riches of God's glory is too high and beyond what we dare think or ask. He knew what the greatness of God's power had done in his own life. He knew God was ready to do a miracle in anyone who would give himself up with his whole heart and life to trust God. He answers every doubt and encourages every sincere soul who is willing to trust God for the fulfillment of the prayer to say with him, "Now unto him that is able to do exceeding abundantly above all that we ask or think, according to the power that worketh in us, Unto him be glory in the church by Christ

Jesus, throughout all ages, world without end. Amen'' (Ephesians 3:20).

Here is Paul's standard of the New Testament life. Is it ours? Do I believe it with my whole heart and soul? Does it inspire my private devotion in the prayer closet? Does it make me realize that my life's devotion is the best and the happiest thing there is in the world?

Who will yield himself, like Paul, to be an intercessor? Who will plead not only with but also for the believers around him, that they may learn to expect the almighty power of God to work in them? What has previously appeared beyond their reach may become the object of their longing desire and their confident assurance—a life of faith in which Christ reigns in their hearts.

Chapter 11

ONE IN THE SPIRIT

"I. . .beseech you that ye walk worthy of the vocation wherewith ye are called, With all lowliness and meekness, with longsuffering, forbearing one another in love; Endeavoring to keep the unity of the Spirit in the bond of peace" (Ephesians 4:1-3).

The letter to the Ephesians is divided into two equal parts. In chapters one through three, we have the divine life in its heavenly origin as revealed in the heart of man by the Holy Spirit. In chapters four through six, we see the Christian life in the ordinary conduct of our daily walk. The two halves correspond to what we said of devotion as an act and as a habit.

The first three chapters begin with adoration: "Blessed be God. . .who hath blessed us" (Ephesians 1:3). They tell us what all those blessings are and end by glorifying Him who is able to do above all that we can ask or think. In every act of prayer and praise, the soul takes its place in the midst of all those riches and seeks to enter more fully into their possession.

The last three chapters begin with an admonition to walk worthy of our high calling. We are taught how to show our devotion as a habit in the common actions of daily life. Devotion lifts us up into the heavenlies to return to this earth charged with blessings. In all our actions, we will prove that our whole life is devoted to God alone.

The Evidence Of Our Calling

The opening words of the second half of the letter bring us down to the roots of the Christian life. The great mark of our high calling is a Christ-like humility. The unity of the Spirit is to be maintained in our relationships with our fellow-believers. Amid all diversity of character and all the temptations arising from the imperfections of those around us, the first mark of a life wholly devoted to God is this: "Walk. . .with all lowliness and meekness."

To realize the full impact of this command, first look at it in its connection with the first three chapters. Think of the heavenly blessings God has given us. Think of the greatness of His power to us who believe and of the Holy Spirit who reveals that power in us. Through Him we have access to God in Christ and are built up as a habitation of God. We are mightily strengthened by Him according to the riches of God's glory so that Christ can dwell in our hearts.

Take time and form a true conception of the wonderful standard of spiritual life indicated in these words. The one fruit of this astonishing revelation of the grace of God and the one mark that you are truly a partaker of it will be a deep and never ceasing humility. Your humility proves that God has revealed Himself to you and brought self and pride down into the dust.

Lowliness and meekness should compromise your attitude toward man as well as toward God. You can have no surer proof that God's spiritual blessings in Christ Jesus have reached and mastered a man than his lowliness and meekness in his relationships with his fellowmen. The greatness of God's power raised us out of the death with Christ Jesus to the throne. This same power makes us, like Christ, willing to wear the servant's robe and do the servant's work. What is impossible with men is possible with God.

Following Jesus' Example

We see the true Christlike disposition in Paul's words to the Philippians: "Let nothing be done through strife or vainglory; but in lowliness of mind let each esteem other better than themselves" (Philippians 2:3). The Master Himself, the meek and lowly Lamb of God commanded us, "Learn of me; for I am meek and lowly in heart" (Matthew 11:29).

Paul emphasizes what he has written by adding, "Let this mind be in you, which was also in Christ

Jesus: Who. . .took upon him the form of a servant. . .and became obedient unto death, even the death of the cross'' (Philippians 2:5,7-8). The self-emptying in the heavenly glory, the form of a servant during His earthly life, and then the humbling death of the cross—this was the mind of Christ. Our salvation is rooted in the spirit and practice of a life like this. Through our lowliness and meekness, as we bear with one another in love, Christ will be magnified and our hearts sanctified. It will become obvious to all that we have been with Jesus.

The heart of a servant diligently works to keep the unity of the Spirit in the bond of peace. It is not what we know or say about the beauty of love, the unity of the Body, and the power of the Holy Spirit that proves the true Christian life. Only through our meekness and lowliness in our daily dealings with our fellow-Christians, even when they tempt and try us, do we show we will sacrifice anything to maintain the unity of the Spirit. Jesus gives the name of *chief* to the servant of all. It may not be easy, but Christ came from heaven to bring humility back to this earth and to work it out in our hearts.

Is the Church teaching the lowliness and meekness of Christ and giving it the place it holds in the will and Word of God? Do we make an effort to maintain this standard of Christian living and keep the unity of the Spirit from being disturbed by pride? In our own search after a deeper spiritual life, is this meekness and lowliness our heart's desire and confident hope?

Let this be the first thing we ask of God—a heart humbled by His infinite love and yielded to His Holy Spirit to work out in us, and in His Body around us, the blessed likeness of Jesus our Lord. By the Spirit's grace, humility can become the habit of a life devoted to God.

Let us not forget to link the thought of a Christ-like lowliness with the Holy Spirit and His power. In the power of the Spirit, Christ humbled Himself on the cross as a sacrifice to God. As we fully yield ourselves to the life of the Spirit, the meekness and lowliness of our Lord can be found in us. Let us believe that He can and will work it in us.

Chapter 12

WORKING TOGETHER IN CHRIST

"There is one body, and one Spirit" (Ephesians 4:4).

In the last chapter, our subject was maintaining the *unity of the Spirit* in our relationships with fellow-Christians. Here our subject is the *Spirit of unity*. The Holy Spirit is the source and the power in which believers, as members of one Body in Christ Jesus, are to minister to each other to build up the Body of Christ.

The knowledge of what the Body of Christ means, the insight into its glory and its purpose, and the fulfilling of the place and ministry to which God has called us in the Body, have a deep connection with spiritual life. To receive the Spirit and the love of Christ means death to every vestige of selfishness. We must surrender our life and love entirely to Christ and His Body. The welfare of every member becomes the supreme object of our desire. Let us try to realize what this Body is in which the blessed Spirit of God seeks to manifest Himself.

Masterpiece Under Construction

We know what a masterpiece of divine workmanship a human body is. Made of dust, it is the instrument through which spiritual life can unfold and express itself. Our human bodies are a parable of the Body of believers with Christ as the Head. God "gave him (Christ) to be the head over all things to the church, Which is his body, the fullness of him that filleth all in all" (Ephesians 1:22-23). The Body is to contain and exhibit the divine fullness as it dwells in Christ. "All the building fitly framed together groweth unto an holy temple in the Lord: In whom ye also are builded together for an habitation of God through the Spirit" (Ephesians 2:21-22).

We are reminded that "Christ also loved the church, and gave himself for it. . . .That he might present it to himself a glorious church, not having spot, or wrinkle, or any such thing" (Ephesians 5:25,27).

An intimate union exists between our body and its head. The power of the head to move and use every member and the readiness of every member to yield itself to assist its fellow-members is only a shadow of that mysterious power which links every believer to Christ. This power places the believer at the disposal of his fellow-believers.

The Body of Christ is the highest revelation of

62

the glory of God. He manifested His power to make a creature of the dust, who had fallen under the power of sin and Satan, become the partaker of the holiness of the blessed Son. The Holy Spirit presides over this work today as He encourages each believer to carry out the eternal purpose— that they all should be one, even as the Father is one with the Son. When the Church yields herself to His divine working, the power of the Holy Spirit can be expected to work unhindered in the Church and in the individual members.

United In Ministry

When He ascended on high, Christ gave His Church the gifts of apostles, prophets, evangelists, pastors, and teachers, "for the perfecting of the saints, for the work of the ministry, for the edifying of the body of Christ" (Ephesians 4:12). The apostles and prophets and pastors are not called to build up the Body of Christ. Their work is the *perfecting of the saints for the ministry* of building up. Every saint is to be trained to take part in building up the Body of Christ. Just as every member of your body helps to build the whole, every believer should know his place and work in the Body of Christ in caring for every other member.

Each one of us needs the other. Each one is to feel linked to the whole Body in the love of the Spirit. A Christian should not only avoid doing anything that is selfish or unloving, but actively yield himself to the Spirit to be the instructor and the comforter of all who are weak.

Then it follows—"Till we all come in the unity of the faith. . .unto a perfect man, unto the measure of the stature of the fullness of Christ" (Ephesians 4:13). Nothing less than maturity is to be the aim of each believer, not only for himself, but for all around him. Then the Body may experience the fullness of Him who fills all in all. We can "grow up into him in all things, which is the head, even Christ: From whom the whole body fitly joined together. . .according to the effectual working in the measure of every part, maketh increase of the body unto the edifying of itself in love" (Ephesians 4:15-16).

The significance of all this in our spiritual life is clear. As long as our prayers only aim at our own perfection and happiness, they defeat themselves. Selfishness prevents the answer. Only in the union with the whole Body will each member be healthy and strong. Building up the Body of Christ in love is vital to our spiritual health.

Let intercession, "with all prayers and supplication in the Spirit. . .for all saints" (Ephesians 6:18), be the proof that the Spirit of unity dwells and prays in us. Let us love the brethren fervently with a pure heart. In our home life, in prayer meetings, and in all our fellowship with God's children, let our love watch over and encourage them. Always remember that we and they are indispensable to each other.

Let the Spirit of unity inspire our secret devotions. Grace will be given to live in unceasing devotion to Christ to build up His glorious Body in love.

Chapter 13

ENJOYING GOD'S PRESENCE

"Grieve not the holy Spirit of God" (Ephesians 4:30).

The words of Isaiah sadly sum up the history of Israel and the whole Old Testament covenant: "They rebelled, and vexed his holy Spirit" (Isaiah 63:10). Stephen's scathing rebuke threw the high priests into a rage: "Ye do always resist the Holy Ghost: as your fathers did, so do ye" (Acts 7:51). In the New Testament, provision was made that this should no longer be the case. God promised His people a new heart and a new spirit. He wrote His law in their hearts and gave them His Spirit, so that they would keep His judgments and do them. (See Hebrews 10:16.)

The Spirit of God's Son is given to live in us and have mastery over us. Grieving Him should no longer be a matter of course. The warning, "Grieve not the holy Spirit," is a promise because what grace commands, it enables us to perform. The believer who seeks to live as one who has been sealed with the Holy Spirit will find that his faith in the power and presence of the Spirit within makes it possible to live without grieving Him.

Perfect Harmony With God

The danger of grieving the Spirit is great unless we live entirely under His power. We need to heed the warning and make a study of all that can possibly hinder His blessed work in us.

The context (from verse 25) speaks of falsehood, anger, stealing, corrupt speech, and transgressions of the law of love. These were to be put far away. Everything that is against God's law grieves His Holy Spirit.

The commands of the Lord Jesus include the beatitudes pronounced on the poor in spirit, the meek, the merciful, and the pure in heart. He taught us to bear the cross, deny self, forsake the world, and follow Him. He instructed His disciples to love one another as He had loved them and to serve one another. These are the marks of the heavenly life Christ came to bring. Everything that is not in harmony with these grieves the Spirit and prevents the enjoyment of His presence.

Paul tells us, "Whatsoever is not of faith is sin" (Romans 14:23). While God's Word announces the major principles of our action, the Holy Spirit teaches the individual believer to apply those principles in daily life. In little things, in doubtful things, in things where opinions differ among

Christians, the believer grieves the Spirit when he does not wait for His guidance and acts contrary to His mind. The whole life of the believer is to be under the Spirit's control with the heart watchful and ready to obey in everything. What is not of faith must be yielded to God at once, or it may become a cloud that darkens the light of the Spirit in His divine tenderness.

Scripture speaks of the struggle between the flesh and the Spirit. It tells us that the only way a believer can live the life in the Spirit is in the power of the truth. "They that are Christ's have crucified the flesh" (Galatians 5:24). Even as Christ yielded His life and His flesh to the death of the cross, so the believer accepts God's judgment on his whole sinful nature as embodied in the flesh. His own will, strength, and even his goodness have been given up to the power of the cross. He says by faith, "I am crucified with Christ. . .Christ liveth in me" (Galatians 2:20). Anything that yields to the flesh hinders and grieves the blessed Spirit. A tender, humble, watchful dependence on the blessed Spirit and His leading is necessary if we are to maintain His fellowship undisturbed.

The Revelation Of Jesus

The great work of the Holy Spirit is to reveal Christ to the believer in the glory of His heavenly life and in His power at work in our hearts. As a preparation for this, His first work is to convict us of the sin of unbelief. The salvation God has prepared for us is complete in Jesus Christ. His life of humility and obedience has been prepared for us and can be received and lived through simple faith alone.

The great secret of the true Christian lies in the daily, unceasing faith in what Jesus will work in us each moment of our life. When this faith is not exercised and sought after, the Christian life becomes feeble. Nothing grieves the Holy Spirit as much as the unbelief which prevents Jesus from showing His power to deliver men from the power of sin and the world.

We need to see the simplicity and the glory of the gospel we profess. In Jesus Christ all that His life, death, and resurrection accomplished is stored up for us. The fullness of life that is in Jesus is reproduced in us, enabling us to grow into the likeness of His humility, love, and obedience.

This is not accomplished by any power in ourselves. The Holy Spirit is given and lives in us to communicate and maintain the life of Christ in the soul. Feel the urgency of the command: "Grieve not the holy Spirit of God." What an unspeakable blessing will come if we yield to Him!

We are in search of the New Testament standard of a life of devotion. Suppose we could ask Paul about his personal experience. He would answer, "I am sure that the child of God, living fully in the power of the Holy Spirit can please God. There is no reason to grieve the Spirit every day."

The different standard of our modern Christianity is simply the result of ignorance and unbelief in the supernatural working of the Spirit in the heart. Paul lived his life of devotion in the fullness and the joy of the Holy Spirit. Is our standard limited because such an experience is seldom taught and lived? Is the reason for this that our knowledge is too intellectual and that the Holy Spirit is not honored as the only Teacher of spiritual truth?

We need to return to the prayer in Ephesians 1:15-23. Let it teach us to receive the Spirit of wisdom as the only Teacher that can enable us to experience the heavenly life God has prepared for us.

Chapter 14

UNLOCKING YOUR SPIRITUAL TREASURE

"Be not drunk with wine. . .but be filled with the Spirit; Speaking to yourselves in psalms and hymns and spiritual songs" (Ephesians 5:18-19).

Grieve not the Spirit! Be filled with the Spirit! All our duty to the Spirit is included in these two commands. The one is negative, forbidding everything of the flesh or self that would lead to unbelief or disobedience to Christ Jesus. The other is positive, calling us to yield our whole being in surrender to Him who reveals and maintains the life of Christ within us.

To understand the command, "Be filled with the Spirit," we need to turn to the day of Pentecost. The disciples were all filled with the Holy Spirit, and we know the dynamic change He worked in their lives. For three years they had lived day and night in close fellowship with their Lord. His presence meant everything to them. When He spoke of His departure, their hearts were sad. He promised that the Spirit would come, not to take His place, but to reveal Himself as their Lord. He would be present with them as much as when He was on earth, only far more intimately and gloriously. He would now live and work in them, even as the Father lived and worked in Him on the earth.

To be filled with the Spirit meant that Christ on the throne would be an ever-present, living reality, filling their hearts and lives with all His heavenly love and joy. Their fellowship with Him on earth proved to be merely the shadow of that intense and unceasing union with Him which the Spirit revealed in power.

Our Part In Pentecost

The command, "Be filled with the Spirit," that all that the disciples received and enjoyed at Pentecost is for us, too. The Church has sunk down from the level of Pentecost to a life in which the spirit of the world and of human wisdom is far too prevalent. Few believe in the possibility of the constant presence of Christ dwelling in the heart and conquering sin. We despair of a life of devotion and perfect self-sacrifice by the fire of His love, guiding us into all His will and work by the leading of His blessed Spirit. The heavenly vision of Christ at the right hand of God, ministering salvation to the penitent and spiritual fulfillment to all He has sanctified, is scarcely known. As the result of this, few witness the greatness of His power toward us who believe.

The condition required for this blessing to be

received can be studied in the disciples. They turned their backs on the world and gave up everything to follow Christ. They had learned to know and love Him and do His will. As our Savior said, "If ye love me, keep my commandments. And I will pray the Father, and he will give you another Comforter" (John 14:15-16).

Jesus' disciples had remained with Him in His temptations. He carried them with Him through death and the grave. The joy and the power of the resurrection life filled their hearts with confidence and hope. Their whole being was yielded up and united with the ascended Lord on the throne. They were fully prepared to receive the wondrous gift that was to come upon them.

The Church of our day is sadly lacking in that separation from the world. The intense attachment and obedience to Christ, the fellowship with His suffering and conformity to His death, and the devotion to Christ on the throne seem almost forgotten. Where is our confident expectation of the never-ceasing flow of living water from the throne of grace which gives the assurance that the fullness of the Spirit will not be withheld? No wonder the mighty power of God is seldom known and felt in our churches!

Aglow With The Spirit

Let us turn once again to Pentecost and think of the great gift that was bestowed. The Spirit made the disciples see that He who had come to dwell in them was indeed the true God. Rivers of life flowed from Him through them and out to the world. Coming fresh from the throne of our Lord in heaven, He rested on them as the Spirit of glory and of God. He filled their hearts with the love and power of Christ in glory. As the mighty power of God dwelling in them, He convinced the world by their boldness and love that God was in their midst.

Most Christians' understanding of the Spirit is far different from the experience of the presence and power of Christ that God desires for us. The thought of the Spirit to them is little more than a mental conception or a passing emotion with a slight sense of power or happiness. Where is the consciousness that fills the soul with deep reverence, quiet rest, heavenly joy, and strength as the natural and permanent possession of the believer?

"Be filled with the Spirit." Before any filling can take place, two things are needed. First, the vessel must be clean, empty, and ready to receive the water that is waiting for it. Then the water must be near and ready to give itself in full measure to the waiting vessel. In the great transaction between God and man for the filling of the Spirit, man needs first of all to know how to surrender completely. The death to self and the world and yielding up the whole being is essential. God is ready and able to take possession of our being and fill us with Himself.

Our Lord Jesus said, "He that believeth on

me. . .out of his belly shall flow rivers of living water" (John 7:38). He named one condition of being filled with the Spirit to overflowing—simple faith in Himself. Faith is not an imagination or an argument or an intellectual conviction. It claims the whole heart and yields up the whole being. It trusts unreservedly in the power that seeks to take possession of it. The blessing is found in the life of faith and cultivated in secret fellowship and wholehearted surrender.

Let us pray that our blessed Lord will deliver us from all that could keep us back from a life of full faith and close fellowship with Him. Answer the call to worship and wait until the Spirit dwells within us, revealing the Father and the Son. He will work in our hearts even what is done in heaven above.

Chapter 15

PREPARED FOR SPIRITUAL WARFARE

"Take. . .the sword of the Spirit, which is the word of God" (Ephesians 6:17).

Paul begins the last section of his letter to the Ephesians with the words, "Finally, my brethren, be strong in the Lord, and in the power of his might" (Ephesians 6:10). In chapter one, he wrote of the "exceeding greatness of his power to us-ward who believe" (v. 19)—the resurrection power which lifted Christ to the throne. Again in chapter three, he spoke of being "strengthened with might by his Spirit in the inner man" (v. 16). Believers are to prove in their lives that all that has been said and written of God's power manifesting itself in His Church is a divine reality. The Spirit is the mighty power of God, and the Spirit-filled Christian should be strong for God's service and the wars of His Kingdom.

Paul tells us, "We wrestle not against flesh and blood, but against principalities, against powers, against the rulers of the darkness of this world, against spiritual wickedness in high places" (Ephesians 6:12). To live victoriously, we must wear the whole armor of God every day and stand strong in Christ and in the strength of His might.

The believer not only has to face various temptations but take his place as one whom Christ leads in warfare against the kingdom of darkness. In the work of the Church, the victory of the cross over the power of Satan is to be carried out in the same power through which Christ triumphed over the grave.

Defense And Offense

When Paul says, "Take unto you the whole armour of God" (Ephesians 6:13) he begins by speaking of the various parts of defensive armor. The Christian first needs to see that he is perfectly safe in the protection of his Lord. Only then is he fit for acting on the offensive. Paul mentions only one weapon of attack—the sword. That sword is the sword of the Spirit, the Word of God.

To know its power and how to use it effectually, we can look to our leader, the Captain of the Lord's host. When Jesus Christ met Satan in the wilderness, He conquered him by the Word of God alone. As a man, He had studied that Word. He loved it, He obeyed it, and He lived in it. The Holy Spirit brought to His mind the familiar words He needed to meet and conquer every Satanic suggestion.

To use the sword of the Spirit in the hour of

battle means that I have lived in that Word and that it abides in me. I have given it the mastery of my whole being. The Spirit of Christ within me enables me by faith to cast out Satan by the Word.

The man who yields his whole being to the Word, who lives by every word that comes from the mouth of God, will be a good soldier of Jesus Christ. In the struggle with doubt and worldliness, with open or secret iniquity, with feeble, hopeless Christians, with dark superstition, nominal Christianity, or a backsliding Church—the Word of God will always be the weapon of victory to those who know how to use it properly.

We learn to use our sword from the vision of John in Patmos. He saw One like the Son of Man, and "out of his mouth went a sharp twoedged sword" (Revelation 1:16).

John heard Him say, "These things saith he which hath the sharp sword with two edges. . . .Repent; or else I will come unto thee quickly, and will fight against them with the sword of my mouth" (Revelation 2:12,16).

Christ has been revealed to us, calling us to repent of sin, especially the sin of our unbelief. He has fought against the evil in us with the sword of His mouth, so that the power of the Word will be revealed in us. Now we can be strong to wield the sword of the Spirit.

"For the word of God is quick, and powerful, and sharper than any twoedged sword, piercing even to the dividing asunder of soul and spirit, and of the joints and marrow, and is a discerner of the thoughts and intents of the heart'' (Hebrews 4:12). The Word shows us the difference between the soulish and spiritual realms. It discovers our most secret intentions and inclinations in the light of God and His holiness. The branch that has been cleansed by the Word will bear much fruit. The soul that has fully yielded itself to the sword of His mouth will have faith and strength to wield it against every enemy.

Mobilized For Battle

Every believer is called to be a soldier in Christ's army. The spiritual powers of darkness are to be met and overcome by all who have learned that they are not to live for themselves, but wholly for Him who redeemed them. Jesus leads them as His conquering forces to rout the spiritual hosts of wickedness in heavenly places. Many Christians have never understood their calling and have never given their lives unreservedly for the one object of securing the triumph of our Redeemer in the world.

Listen to the summons that calls us to the war. Let us confess and repent that we seldom stand in the strength of the Lord and in the power of His might, with our armor on day and night. Let our ears be opened to the call that comes from every Church for men and women who will yield themselves to Christ for His service, whether in the home or on the mission field.

We are to prove first in our own life that God's Word has power with Him in prayer and intercession, and with us in surrender and cleansing. There we learn to use it. Our love for our Lord and for souls will rouse us to the war. The Word of God will become the sword of the Spirit that we carry to meet the enemy and to deliver his captives.

How helpless is the Church of our day with its thousands of missionaries to meet the needs of millions of unbelievers. How strong it might be if every believer were trained to yield to the two-edged sword proceeding out of the mouth of the Son of Man. After it has done its work in his own heart, he could grasp it and use it to bring deliverance to those who are dying in bondage to sin.

Our private devotions have often been the vain attempt to find nourishment or joy in the Word of God. We failed because our first thought was the selfish one of seeking comfort or holiness for ourselves. Let us repent and learn that a Christian is saved so that Christ may use him for the welfare of the whole Body and of those who have not yet been gathered into it.

May our devotions bear these two simple marks—the entire surrender to the Word of God as the two-edged sword and the surrender to wield that two-edged sword in the power of the Holy Spirit against every enemy of Christ and His Kingdom.

Chapter 16

VICTORY THROUGH INTERCESSION

"Praying always with all prayer and supplication in the Spirit, and watching thereunto with all perseverance and supplication for all saints" (Ephesians 6:18).

The Christian's wrestling is against the spiritual hosts of wickedness in the heavenly places. He must put on his armor and wield the sword of the Spirit in complete dependence on God and with confidence in His all-sufficient grace. A life of constant prayer is the secret of a life of victory. Praying in the Spirit is the mark of the normal spiritual life.

Our lungs are kept breathing by the divine power which upholds our physical life. Likewise, the Holy Spirit will certainly breathe in us that prayer which maintains the powers of the divine life and the heavenly world. Salvation is not accomplished by works or struggling. We are God's workmanship, "created in Christ Jesus unto good works, which God hath before ordained that we should walk in them" (Ephesians 2:10). The Bible tells us that we are a divine creation, not finished and left to ourselves, but with every moment of our lives upheld by the Word of His power. Unceasing prayer is possible and is commanded because the eternal Spirit causes it to become the heavenward breathing of the soul.

What Should We Pray For?

Praying at all times is by no means to be selfish, referring only to our own needs. "Watching thereunto with all perseverance and supplication *for all the saints.*" Paul taught us the importance of unity in the Body of Christ in love. In contrast to the wrestling of believers with the powers of darkness, he speaks of the unity of the saints as they form one great army of the Lord. This army has been made alive by one spirit and is striving together to establish His Kingdom in the world. Continual earnest prayer for all believers is not only our duty, but it is vital for the welfare and the victory of the whole Body.

We can learn the subject of our prayers from Paul's own petitions. In chapter one, he prayed for those who had already been sealed with the Spirit. He asked that God would give them the Spirit of wisdom and divine illumination that they might know the greatness of His power in all who believe.

Believers need to allow this great truth to take hold of their hearts and thoroughly possess them.

Those who have sought this for themselves need to be reminded of their calling to make this request for others. The health of the Church as a whole and the spiritual strength of individual believers or churches depends on our perseverance in prayer for all the saints.

True believers need the prayers of other believers. The prayer is to be specific, pleading for the Spirit of divine power to fill their inner man, that Christ may dwell in their hearts and that they be rooted in love. All believers are to unite in pleading for all the saints.

The Secret Of Revival

Prayer is to be marked by perseverance. Praying always in the Spirit for all saints is the secret of true revival in God's children. The minister who is pleading as an intercessor for his congregation also needs their prayers in return. As blood is purified by the fresh air we breathe, even so the Spirit of prayer breathes in the air of heaven and breathes up to heaven the unceasing supplication of love. This is essential to the health of the Body of Christ, and the work of the ministry depends on it.

The minister should teach believers that intercession is one of their highest privileges. The work of the missionary who, like Paul, carries the gospel to the ungodly depends on it. New power would fill our mission work if believers answered the call to pray at all times in the Spirit. Grace would be given to Christian workers as they boldly proclaim the mystery of the gospel. Preaching the Word to the wise or to the ignorant, to the Greek or the Jew, reveals Christ—the power of God and the wisdom of God.

Paul gives us a great vision of the work to be done in our daily hour of devotion. We see the hosts of spiritual wickedness in heavenly places and Jesus Christ ruling over all and carrying out the triumph of the cross. Victory is won as the members of Christ labor together and wrestle in preaching and in prayer for the conquest of the world. Our devotions take on a new meaning and glory as we grow strong in the Lord and the power of His might. We will no longer live for ourselves and our religious hopes and efforts but live in love, even as Christ loved us. Each believer can learn to give himself as an offering to God for the building up of the Body of Christ.

May God help us to catch the fire of inspiration that Paul's letter to the Ephesians holds out to us. We can know the rewards of praying always in the Spirit for all the saints, and above all, for the ministers of the gospel.

Chapter 17

FULFILLED IN GOD'S PLAN

"God. . .hath blessed us with all spiritual blessings in heavenly places in Christ" (Ephesians 1:3).

In Paul's letter to the Ephesians, the expression, "the heavenly places," is used five times. In the heavenly places, God blessed us with every spiritual blessing in Christ. He set Christ at His right hand and made us sit with Christ. The wisdom of God is to be made known through the Church to principalities and powers. We are ready to wrestle against the spiritual hosts of wickedness. No man or woman can live a Christian life except in the power of the heavenly world.

In his excellent letter, Paul reveals the mystery of God's will and His purpose in Christ. He helps us understand our resurrection and ascension with Christ, our new creation, and our glory as a part of the Body of Christ. As the light of the Holy Spirit shines on one truth after another, we learn how truly divine and heavenly our life on earth can be.

Knowing Our Heavenly Calling

We have studied the twelve passages in which the Holy Spirit is mentioned. Let us gather all their teaching into one and see if we can sketch a portrait of the man called to live by this heavenly standard.

The believer has been sealed in Christ by the Holy Spirit of promise. The Spirit is the down payment of his inheritance, the pledge of what he is and can become in Christ, and the divine assurance that every promise can be fulfilled. He has the seal of God on his forehead, and his whole being bears the stamp of the Holy Spirit.

The first blessing of the Spirit is that He enlightens our eyes to know our calling and the greatness of God's power to fulfill His plan in us. The Holy Spirit reveals God's power in raising Christ from the dead of the throne of glory as the pledge of what God will work in us each day.

The sealed one has been brought near to God by the blood of His Son and lives in the Holy Place. Through the Spirit he has a life of perfect fellowship with God in Christ Jesus.

The sealed one no longer lives for himself but as a member of the great spiritual temple built for God through the Spirit. The Spirit links the believer to the chief cornerstone and to all his fellow-saints. He also knows the mystery of Christ among the Gentiles and counts them as fellow-heirs to all the unsearchable riches of Christ. He lives for the Kingdom and the conversion of the unbelievers as Christ's inheritance.

The sealed one has learned that only by God's almighty power can he live in the heavenly places. He continually prays that the power of the Spirit may strengthen him mightily. He wants Christ to dwell in his heart by faith and to be filled with love and with all the fullness of God. He asks for himself and for others that God may reveal His Son in them.

The sealed one bears the image of Jesus. He walks worthy of his heavenly calling, humbly maintaining the unity of the Spirit. He knows he can do this because God strengthens him with might in the inner man. His calling is to minister to the saints and build up the Body of Christ in love.

Above everything else, he seeks never to grieve the Holy Spirit of God. In this way, he can partake of all the blessings in the heavenly places in Christ. He cultivates a tender spirit.

Walking In The Spirit

The more the believer knows about the sealing of the Spirit and the work that He does, the greater is his desire to yield himself completely to the Spirit's control. At the same time, he feels the need of a deeper vision of the riches of grace dispensed by the blessed Spirit. He sees that to be filled with the Spirit means peace, joy, health, and strength.

The seal of the Spirit includes the call to be a soldier and to be strong in the Lord and the power of His might. The believer understands that divine power is promised him so that he may wrestle against the powers of evil with the sword of the Spirit and rescue men for Christ and His service. He obeys the call to a life of continual prayer with perseverance for all saints and for all ministers of the Word. The Spirit makes it possible for him to be a true soldier and prayer warrior.

"Blessed be the God and Father of our Lord Jesus Christ, who hath blessed us with all spiritual blessings in heavenly places in Christ" (Ephesians 1:3). Let us meditate on the blessings until we realize what a glorious salvation God has prepared for us. A believer who is sealed by the Spirit is taught to know the divine power working in him. He enjoys perfect fellowship with the Father, united with all his fellow-saints as the temple of God.

Strengthened with might by the Spirit, Christ dwells in his heart, and he is filled with all the fullness of God. He walks in all meekness and lowliness in his daily life, keeping the unity of the Spirit. In the power of the Spirit he works to build up the Body in love. He hungers to be filled with the Spirit and never grieves Him. He fulfills the law of love in his daily life and is strong in the Lord and the power of His might to wrestle with the powers of darkness, using the Word and praying for all saints.

It takes time, thought, prayer, and quiet waiting on the Spirit of God for anyone to keep the vision of the Spirit-sealed, Spirit-taught, Spirit-strengthened, and Spirit-filled believer. We must turn from self and the world to allow God to work in us according to the counsel of His own will.

Let us not forget our purpose in studying Paul's letter to the Ephesians. Let us believe in the divine standard of the Christian life it sets before us. By the almighty power of God alone, it can become ours. If we are serious about seeking deliverance from worldly standards, we can count on the infinite mercy of God to work in us what otherwise appears to be utterly hopeless—a life filled with the Spirit.

Chapter 18

BECAUSE OF UNBELIEF

"Why could not we cast him out? And Jesus said unto them, Because of your unbelief" (Matthew 17:19-20).

Do you think it is possible to carry out the Ephesian standard of spirituality in your own daily life? Some people would say that they do not see how it can be possible because of the sin in every believer that makes daily confession absolutely necessary. Others might answer that although such a standard is possible for Paul and other spiritual men, it is not within the reach of all. Such a life is not for everyone. A large majority content themselves with the thought of an attractive yet unattainable ideal which exercises its elevating influence on those who remain far below it.

Surely Paul meant in all sincerity not only to testify of what God had shown him by revelation, but had actually accomplished within him. He speaks in chapter one of the revelation of the Spirit to make us know the greatness of God's power through our faith in Christ raised from the dead and seated on the throne. In chapter three he tells of our being strengthened by the Spirit in the inner man, so that the great miracle of grace is perfected in us. Christ dwells in our heart, filling us with all the fullness of God. He finally adds the ascription of praise, "Now unto him that is able to do exceeding abundantly above all that we ask or think, according to the power that worketh in us, Unto him be glory" (Ephesians 3:20-21). Paul undoubtedly means that this was his own experience, and he confidently urges his readers to believe that it can be theirs.

An Ideal Or An Experience?

The greatness of God's power working in the heart from moment to moment, day by day, is the ground on which the standard of devotion rests. Paul holds this standard out to us. Unceasing prayer is required to know this power, to believe it, and to receive it. Without prayer, we will regard the standard as an impractical one and continue in ignorance of what is offered for our acceptance.

Why is this mighty power of God working in us seldom taught and rarely experienced? Is the whole Church in error in resting content with a far lower standard than what Paul's letter holds out to us? The answer to these questions will lead us to the root of the evil from which the Church is suffering.

We all know God gave Abraham to Israel as the great example of faith in Him. Abraham believed that God was able to raise the dead, both in his own case and in the sacrifice of Isaac. Yet we know how Israel, from the beginning of God's dealings in Egypt, continually grieved Him by unbelief. Their unbelief condemned them to forty years of wandering in the wilderness. Psalm 78 tells us their story and shows how they continually limited God by unbelief.

We know, too, how our Lord Jesus continually sought to cultivate faith in His disciples as the one condition for them seeing the power and the glory of God. He set Paul forth as a witness to the power of faith, not only in justification, but in the whole of our spiritual life and service.

Yet just as Israel, despite the example of Abraham, utterly failed in trusting God, so in the Church it became plain how little man knows to receive his salvation based on trust in God alone. We know how terribly the Galatians failed. The letter to the Hebrews warns above everything against unbelief. The Church of the second century was brought into bondage under the law. The human heart naturally turns from grace and faith to the law and works.

In the lives of the Church fathers we find, with all their earnestness, how little they understood faith in the power of God as the one secret of a life pleasing to Him. They developed a religion in which the grace of God was connected with the confession of endless sins. The voice of Paul and his faith in God's mighty keeping and saving power was seldom heard. The generations that heard the gospel of justification by faith hardly understood that sanctification is also by faith. The power of a holy life for victory over the world and the flesh can only be found in an unceasing exercise of faith in the greatness of God's power in us. We should not be surprised that one of the great causes of feebleness in the Church today is the unbelief in the mighty power of Jesus.

Reasons For Power Failure

We often hear complaints of the lack of power in the Church. It seems unprepared to guide its members to true devotion to Christ and to influence the unsaved multitude around us. The chief cause of all is often overlooked—a Church that does not experience the power of Christ dwelling in the hearts of His people to overcome the power of sin cannot expect that mighty power in its conflict with Satan and his hosts.

The first great work of the Holy Spirit is to convict people of their unbelief. Where that work has not been fully done, nothing will happen until the Church confesses that all its weakness is due to this one thing—not giving Christ His place of honor. Jesus said, "All power is given unto me in heaven and in earth" (Matthew 28:18). As the Church believes and experiences this, it will learn to expect Him to do His mighty works.

Ask yourself the question: Do I believe in the power of God in Christ by His Spirit to work in me the life depicted in this epistle? Instead of mourning over the sins we cannot master, the pride, self-will, lack of love, or disobedience, let us come to the root of the matter and confess our terrible sin of unbelief. Let our faith grow in the greatness of God's power revealed in Christ. We will be strengthened by the Spirit with might and led on to the fullness of God. As we humble ourselves before God in the confession of our unbelief, He will reveal Christ in us. Our life can indeed become the response to the divine call: "Be strong in the Lord, and in the power of his might" (Ephesians 6:10).

Chapter 19

HARMONY BETWEEN GOD AND MAN

"Who then can be saved? And he said, The things which are impossible with men are possible with God" (Luke 18:26-27).

The great hindrance to the power of God's Word in the truth we have found in Ephesians is the thought—*God's standard is an impossible one.* Our only response to this doubt must be to listen again to the voice of Christ as He tells us that what is impossible with man is possible with God. God can do for us what appears to be beyond His reach and ours. God can work in us what He worked in Paul.

What is implied in the great gift of the Holy Spirit? No word is used in such a variety of ways as the word *spirit.* It can mean anything in which the mind of man exerts and proves its power, or it can mean the highest revelation of God's holiness and love. The same word is used, increasing the danger that each person will only understand it according to his own point of view. We often suffer from our defective view of what is really meant by the Spirit of God and of Christ.

God sent His Son into the world as a man so that He would work out in His life a holy nature. This nature could then be imparted to believers in Christ as a thing already prepared and brought into existence for us. Just as the grain of wheat dies and reappears in the full ear of corn with its hundredfold reproduction of the seed, Christ died that He may live again in our lives here on earth.

When Jesus ascended to the throne, the Father gave Him the Spirit to pour down His life in the hearts of His people. The Spirit communicates the holy nature of Christ with a divine power to all who believe. They live by the Spirit and are led by the Spirit. The Spirit is their life.

Working With God

In the wonderful union of the divine and the human life in the believer, everything depends on the true relationship being maintained between God and man. God works all in all, and man receives all from God to work it out in trust and obedience. Where this relationship is not properly understood, man will use his own effort to take the place that God wants to fill. He thinks that if he can secure God's help in his efforts, he has found the path to holiness and growth. He does not understand that the Spirit must have absolute control, and he must exercise direct and unceasing dependence on Him.

Two men may be praying that God would give them the Spirit of wisdom. The one may be thinking only of the ordinary measures of help he has connected with the thought of the Spirit. But the other is expecting that God will do more than he can ask or think.

The great secret of the Christian life is found in dying to self and being brought to nothing by the cross of Christ. Before our Lord Jesus could receive the new life from the Father and impart the gift of the Holy Spirit to His people, He had to give up the life He lived on earth. He had to take His place among the dead in weakness and helplessness before He could live again by the power of God. His death on the cross was indispensable to the life of the Spirit.

As it was with Christ, so it must be with us. As we yield ourselves to be united with Him in the likeness of His death, we can share with Him in the glory and power of the life of the Spirit. To know what the Holy Spirit means implies knowing what death means. The cross and the Spirit are inseparable. The soul that understands that death to self is the gate to true life is ready to learn what and who the Holy Spirit is.

Why is our understanding of what the Holy Spirit can and will do for us so limited? The great mark of the New Testament Church was the presence of the Holy Spirit in power. Today we only see a feeble representation of the Spirit's work. Our conversions, preaching, fellowship, life, aggressive work for God and His Kingdom—everywhere it is obvious that the power of the Spirit is seldom known.

Endless discussions and efforts are made to lift our churches to a higher level and to convince people to accept the truth of God's Word. But there has not yet been, on the part of the Church as a whole, anything like the intense and sorrowful confession that, as churches and as Christians, we have grieved the Spirit of God. Our calling is to honor Him and to prove by His presence in our life that Christ is indeed Lord.

The Source Of Spiritual Blessings

In the epistle to the Ephesians, the Holy Spirit takes an important place. Paul must have had some reason for saturating the letter with the truth of the Spirit's presence and work. The epistle to the Colossians was written about the same time, and it carries the same theme. Yet there is one very marked difference. In Colossians the Holy Spirit is mentioned only once, but in Ephesians He is mentioned twelve times. Paul felt the need to express a system of truth in which the presence and power of the Holy Spirit is evident in the life of the Christian.

Let us make certain that when we think of the Holy Spirit, we mean what God means. He means the Holy Spirit, God the Spirit, God the Holy One, God in His holiness living within us. In Him we have the whole God, not only His power, but the living God Himself. We need to allow our whole man, spirit, soul, and body, to be possessed and controlled by Him. As we think of what God in the Spirit is willing to do in us, we will realize that only we can keep Him from doing His work in us. We must get rid of ourselves, lose our life, and die with Christ. Our new nature made alive in Him will be the fit vessel for all the blessing the Spirit will bring.

Chapter 20

GIVING GOD THE GLORY

"Now unto him that is able to do exceeding abundantly above all that we ask or think, according to the power that worketh in us, unto him be glory"(Ephesians 3:20-21).

In any discussion on Paul's letter to the Ephesians, we should emphasize the power of God and the place it is meant to take in the life of the Christian. All that we have learned about the Holy Spirit cannot have its full effect in our lives without a complete surrender to the almighty working of God's power. Believers need to have an intense, personal, and abiding faith that God's power must be known and honored as the secret of living according to the New Testament standard. God will enlighten us by His Spirit that we may know the greatness of His power within us.

Paul gives special emphasis to the thought that our salvation is the result of the direct working of God's almighty power. He speaks of "the purpose of him who worketh all things after the counsel of his own will" (Ephesians 1:11). God does this, not only with regard to the great work of deliverance in Christ, but also in every detail in the daily life of the Christian. We think of Him as the omnipotent One, able to work mightily when He chooses. But the words suggest something far greater. God works every moment, not only in nature with its every leaf and flower, but in His children, too. He provides all that they need for carrying out His blessed will.

Power Working In You

Nothing less than the power of the Father's might that raised Christ from the dead can meet the daily needs of your soul and accomplish what God longs to see in you. The Holy Spirit gives you spiritual insight into the greatness of His power and enables you to know that God is working in you. Then He will be able to do for you what He has not yet done.

The Christian strives after the life that the Word puts before him. He prays that God would aid him in his weakness, but he fails to understand that only the greatness of God's power in him can do the work. "The weakness of God is stronger than man" (1 Corinthians 1:25). The strength of God is only found in the consciousness of utter weakness.

This was the mark of the working of the might of His power in Christ. Our Lord died, sinking down into absolute weakness, without a vestige of the power of thought or will. He yielded Himself to the Father, and God's power raised Him out of absolute weakness to the place of power on the throne. Only the teaching of the Holy Spirit can enable us to know the greatness of God's power working in us.

As this thought masters us, we will understand the standard of the life Paul puts before us. By divine power, God will work in us to give us the courage to see and live a life pleasing to Him in every way.

Paul speaks of the grace of God given to him "by the effectual working of his power" (Ephesians 3:7). He experienced and counted on this direct working of God for all the grace he needed for his ministry. He says in Colossians, "I also labour, striving according to his working, which worketh in me mightily" (Colossians 1:29). The man who believes in the working of God's power will cease seeking strength in himself. His whole attitude will be that of simple dependence and perfect trust in God.

God's Almighty Power

The more we strive to take in these thoughts, the better we will understand why Paul again returns to the working of God's almighty power. In chapter one he spoke of the Spirit's enlightenment to show us that the power that raised Christ is needed to work in us in every moment of our spiritual life. In chapter three he goes further and prays that the greatness of God's power according to the riches of His glory may be given to us as an actual strengthening with might by His Spirit in the inner man. Take time and think what that means! The whole spiritual life can be permanently quickened with divine power. Then the indwelling of Christ in the heart will become a divine reality.

The Church has almost lost the concept of the indwelling of Christ as a continual experience. Before this can become part of our living faith and experience, we must see the greatness of God's power that raised Christ from the dead as part of the inheritance of every Christian. The Holy Spirit is the pledge of our inheritance.

Paul realized the importance of the divine power as the one condition of the full spiritual life. The doxology he adds gives God glory just for this one thing—that He is able to do "exceeding abundantly above all that we ask or think." Other attributes of God—His love, His righteousness, His holiness—give us reasons to bless His name. But as the groundwork of all, His almighty power must be our only confidence in all that He is to do in us in carrying out His purpose.

Let us worship and adore Him. Every thought of what is to be done in us, in the Church, and in the world is summed up in the promise, "Able to do exceeding abundantly above all that we ask or think, according to the power that worketh in us!"

Paul closes all his instruction in the epistle with the conclusion: "Finally, my brethren, be strong in the Lord, and in the power of his might" (Ephesians 6:10). He used the same word in Ephesians 1:19, "according to the working of his mighty power;" and in Ephesians 3:16 "to be strengthened with might by his Spirit in the inner man."

This power and strength was meant to be the standard of devotion in those Ephesian Christians. It will become the standard of our devotion when we learn to cast all our weakness at His feet and believe with childlike assurance in the greatness of His power toward us. We will then be prepared to experience a life strong in the Lord and in the power of His might.